I0476949

101
Business
Writing Prompts

Heidi Thorne

Copyright © 2015 Heidi Thorne
All rights reserved.
ISBN: 1522939547
ISBN-13: 978-1522939542

LIMIT OF LIABILITY/DISCLAIMER OF WARRANTY

Heidi Thorne, Thorne Communications LLC, any of its affiliates, and any of its or its affiliate's respective shareholders, directors, officers, employees, agents, representatives, successors or assigns (collectively, "Thorne") does not make any guarantee or other promises as to any results that may be achieved or obtained through your use of the product you've purchased (the "Product") or any information or materials presented therewith, provided in connection therewith or included therein. The information provided in the Product and any accompanying material is for informational purposes only, and should not be used as a substitute for your own research and due diligence. Your use of the Product is at your own risk. You are responsible for checking with appropriate authorities to ensure compliance with all applicable laws and regulations.

Without limiting the foregoing, Thorne hereby disclaims any and all representations and warranties with respect to the Product, including, without limitation, any representation and warranty with respect to the achievement of any results, the correctness or completeness of any information or materials presented with the Product, provided in connection with the Product or included in the Product or the advisability of any act or failure to act. You acknowledge and agree that Thorne shall have no liability or obligation to you or any of your affiliates or any of your or your affiliate's respective shareholders, directors, officers, employees, agents, representatives, successors or assigns for any claims, damages, expenses or other losses arising out of, in connection with, resulting from or otherwise relating to the Product, including, without limitation, any errors or omissions therein.

First Edition: 2015

Thorne Communications LLC
www.HeidiThorne.com

101
Business
Writing Prompts

Heidi Thorne

TABLE OF CONTENTS

WELCOME TO THE CREATIVE WORKOUT FOR YOUR BRAIN!

Do any of these sound like you?

- *You're totally turned on by the idea of writing a book for your business, but you need some creative sparks to get your mind going.*
- *You're scared to write anything—especially for business—because you don't feel that you're good at it (or as good as you want to be).*
- *When you do eek out some time to write, you don't know what to write about. So you end up writing nothing.*
- *You've gotten a little rusty in the writing department and just want to get those creative juices flowing again.*
- *You hated writing in high school or college because it was just useless drudgery. But now you need, even want, to do it as a way to better connect with customers, colleagues and the communities you serve.*
- *You need some new ideas for blog posts since what you've been doing lately is borrrrrring (yes, that's exactly how you'd say it).*

If any of the above describe you, you've got a good case of Writer's Block for your business book or blog. And the writing workout that follows is for YOU!

Like any other muscle or skill, learning to write books or blogs to build your business takes patience and practice... lots of practice. Also, it's not just any old practice that makes perfect. It's the right kind of practice. Developing written thoughts that help you showcase your expert status and thought leadership takes more than writing a few witty words on Facebook or Twitter.

But let's face it. You really don't want to take a writing course (or two or three) at the local college, do you? That's up to 12 or 16 weeks of classes and coursework per course on top of your regular work, kids' homework, housework, yard work and physically working out... not to mention the dollar cost. You want to be able to bring yourself one step closer to launching or resurrecting writing for your book or blog without making it another "career" to add to your already overcommitted life.

So that's why I've developed this course made up of bite-size exercises using a creativity tool used by many professional writers and authors: writing prompts. Briefly, prompts give you a topic to wrap your mind around so that you're not facing a blank sheet of paper or computer screen, wondering what you should write about.

Some prompts will be serious. Others will be more fun. But all prompt exercises are designed to build your creativity and thinking skills for writing business books or blogs. And you're going to develop a lot of crazy, half-baked ideas, some of which won't be ready for primetime. That's okay. Remember, this is exercise and practice, not the actual show.

When I've participated in writing prompt workshops, I've found that even if I don't generate a publication-worthy piece of writing, I usually come up with ideas for other writing I'm doing or even new, totally unrelated projects. I'm sure you'll also find that these exercises will jog your creativity in ways that may surprise you, too.

Let's get started!

Heidi Thorne

PART I:
HOW TO USE WRITING PROMPTS TO BUILD YOUR SKILLS

CHAPTER 1:
What are Writing Prompts?

Looking for a way to boost your creativity and get your mental motor running when it comes to writing? Here's a tool you can use: *writing prompts*.

Writing prompts are short, thought provoking statements or questions that provide a topic on which to write. Some prompts may start with a sentence or a few paragraphs which ask the writer to finish the thought or expand on the topic. Prompts may be categorized by overall topic or genre, such as business, poetry, novel writing, etc. Additionally, some prompt programs may encourage writers of one genre to try an unfamiliar or uncomfortable genre in order to expand the writers' horizons of possibilities and mental flexibility. For example, business nonfiction writers may be encouraged to try poetry or short stories to improve their writing style and audience appeal.

A writing prompt exercise may specify that the writer write a certain amount of words on the prompt topic within a limited time period. In a workshop setting, that time may be as little as a few minutes. For lower pressure, self-directed exercises, writers can usually choose their own time for completion, be it minutes, hours, days or weeks.

Here's how prompts can help build writing skills:

- *They can force the writer to dig deeper mentally or emotionally to address the topic.*
- *For writers that lack focus, they can help quiet distracting thoughts and influences.*
- *Writers sometimes fall into a rut or dry spell. Prompts can help keep up momentum by keeping new topics bubbling into consciousness and encouraging experimentation.*

CHAPTER 2:
How to Develop Your Writing Skills with Prompts

"How Often Should I Do the Prompt Exercises?"

Daily: Good for those who are anxious to develop their skills and momentum quickly. The 101 exercises in this book would provide you with three to five months' worth of exercises, depending on if you write on the weekends or not.

Weekly: Completing one exercise per week is a more comfortable pace for those who have a slew of other obligations and limited time. For a weekly writing schedule, it would take you around two years to get through every exercise in the book.

Switch exercise frequency if you feel you're going too fast or slow for your needs.

"How Long Should I Take to Do Each Exercise?"

You'll want to decide in advance what actual amount of minutes or hours you'll want to devote to each exercise per day.

As noted earlier, in a workshop setting, writers can be given as little as a few minutes to complete an entire exercise. I've experienced deadlines of 5 to 15 minutes in these events! That's definitely for more advanced writers. Outside of this intense workshop setting, the following time limits would be practical:

Daily: Setting aside 15 to 60 minutes per day to complete a single exercise would be a challenging enough time limit for most writers. Keeping it to one hour or less keeps it from overtaking your day.

Weekly: As with a daily schedule, 15 to 60 minutes per day is about the maximum amount of time you'll probably want to devote to working on a single exercise within a week's time. At that pace, you would be giving yourself a total of up to 7 hours to complete one exercise within a 7-day week timeframe.

"How Many Words Should I Write?"

While any of the prompts could, literally, launch an idea for an entire book, start with a manageable goal such as 350 to 500 words per prompt. This is a common word count range for blog posts. If the prompt topic inspires you, go for whatever number of words you can within your designated time limit. If it's a topic that is high value or potential for you, you can return to it at some point in the future to develop it further.

"Where and when should I write?"

Anywhere you feel comfortable! For me, I'm able to get my best ideas flowing when I'm away from my office, such as while relaxing at a coffee shop. For you, it might be at home. Or maybe it would be the first thing you do as you sit down to your desk in the morning. The only caveat is to do it where and when you can get some distraction-free space and time.

However, don't be surprised if you come up with brain spurts throughout your day for an exercise you worked on previously. This is just how the creative brain works sometimes. Always have a notepad and pen, voice recorder or dictation app handy to capture those fleeting inspirations. (Just NOT while you're driving, walking, etc.! Safety first with eyes and attention on the road or whatever you're doing!) Then add those musings to the exercise later.

Yield Not to Temptation

As you begin scanning "Part II: The Business Writing Prompts Exercises" segment of this book, it'll be tempting to bounce around from one exercise to the next because, of course, the next exercise always looks more exciting than the one you're working on right now.

Granted, there may be exercises which are completely inappropriate for you, your line of work or business. It's okay to skip over those. However, do your best to work through each relevant prompt in the lineup and resist the temptation to keep skipping around or ahead.

In addition to completing one exercise before moving on to the next, also avoid trying to work on more than one at a time. That will drain your creative energy and cause you to lose focus.

Don't Obsess, Don't Stop

Perfectionists out there will have a hard time with this! For particularly difficult prompt topics, the temptation is to keep working on that exercise until it's publication worthy. While your commitment to excellence is laudable, this will usually keep you stuck on one exercise and then you've passed up the opportunity to spend time on more suitable topics for you.

Granted, if the difficult prompt topic is relevant to you, your business and goals, it might warrant some extra time working on it and/or thinking about why it's causing you difficulty. But it's probably better to just keep moving forward with the next exercise as scheduled.

Assess Your Progress

You'll want to periodically check in with yourself to assess how you're feeling about the progress your making… or not.

Throughout the prompts exercises in Part II, you'll see Writing Progress Update Exercises. These are just as important as any of the actual writing prompt exercises you do. In fact, you may find them even more challenging!

When you land on one of the Writing Progress Updates, use that as your writing prompt exercise for the day or week.

CHAPTER 3:
What to Do with What You Write

While some ideas that may be spawned by a writing prompt exercise can be the basis for an entire blog post or book, many will not be ready for public viewing now... or ever. That's really okay! Creativity can be a messy business.

But you may be generating some quality ideas and usable material every time you do a prompt exercise. So what should you do with all of it?

Archive

If you write your exercises directly in this workbook, you'll be able to turn to this book as an idea resource in the future. If you decide to handwrite your exercises with separate paper and pen, filing your work in categorized physical folders will help you locate the piece you're looking for more easily.

But if you write your exercises electronically, use categorized folders on your computer, productivity apps such as Evernote, online "cloud" storage systems such as Dropbox, etc. to create an easily searchable archive for future reference.

Regardless of whether you go old school with paper and pen or new school with electronic tools, categorizing, tagging and giving these pieces descriptive titles will help you more easily find the bit you want. For example, don't tag your exercise, "Exercise October 23." Something like "Business Planning for Success" would be easier to identify.

Get Friendly Feedback

You could ask a friend or colleague for feedback. **Caution!** To prevent theft of ideas, make sure to get reviews from only trusted sources who will respect and protect your copyrighted material.

Enhance Your Business and Marketing Strategies

A side benefit of this program is that many of the questions push you to think more deeply about your business or industry. These probing prompts can reveal some rich insights you can apply to your business and marketing strategies.

Hire an Editor to Assess Your Work

Sometimes we're too close to our own work to see the threads, themes and value in it. Hire a content or development editor who can help you evaluate your work for its message, market potential and opportunities for further development into books or blogs.

PART II:
THE BUSINESS WRITING PROMPTS EXERCISES

JOURNAL IT! You can use the lined space provided to write out your entire exercise, similar to how you might write in a journal.

OR

NOTE IT! Write down your thoughts about the topic in the lined spaces provided. Then use a word processing program or app, or a dictation-to-text program (i.e. Dragon), to actually write out your exercise.

1. How would you explain what you do to a 5-year old?

2. If you could pick one thing that your customers don't understand about your business, product or service—but you wish they did—what would that be? Why do they not understand? How could you help them better understand this?

3. If you are not working with the direct decision maker in a customer's organization (or family for consumer products and services), how could you help your contact present your story to those who have authority over the sale?

_____

_____

_____

_____

_____

_____

_____

_____

_____

_____

_____

_____

_____

_____

_____

_____

_____

_____

_____

_____

_____

_____

_____

_____

_____

_____

_____

_____

_____

_____

_____

4.   What makes a person a respected professional in your industry? Be as specific as possible, i.e., answers emails within 24 hours, has well established relationships with vendors, etc.

_____

_____

_____

_____

_____

5. Does your industry or profession have a negative image, in spite of the value offered? Why has that image developed? How could you help reverse that negativity for potential customers or employees?

_____

_____

_____

_____

_____

_____

_____

_____

_____

_____

_____

_____

_____

_____

_____

_____

_____

_____

_____

_____

_____

_____

_____

_____

_____

_____

_____

_____

_____

_____

_____

_____

_____

_____

6. Identify 10 things customers need to know about buying the type of product or service you sell BEFORE they contact you.

7. Apathy is one of the biggest sales challenges for businesses of all types. Why do customers not care about the products or services you (or your industry) offer? How can you break through and help them understand the value?

_____

_____

_____

_____

_____

_____

_____

_____

_____

_____

_____

_____

_____

_____

_____

_____

_____

_____

_____

_____

_____

_____

_____

_____

_____

_____

_____

_____

_____

_____

_____

_____

_____

_____

_____

8. Are there scenarios where customers should NOT buy your product or service? If so, what are they and why?

9. If your business was a music or movie genre (action/adventure, mystery, romantic comedy, easy listening, rock & roll, etc.), what would it be? Why?

10. Centuries from now, an archaeologist is digging up our current civilization and lands upon an artifact or written work by or about you or your business. What would the archaeologist find out about, you, your business and your impact on the world?

_____

_____

_____

_____

_____

_____

_____

_____

_____

_____

_____

_____

_____

_____

_____

_____

_____

_____

_____

_____

_____

_____

_____

_____

_____

_____

_____

_____

_____

_____

_____

_____

_____

WRITING PROGRESS UPDATE #1

CONGRATULATIONS! You made it through the first 10 Writing Prompt Exercises! Be proud of what you've done so far. Let's see how you're feeling about your progress...

Which of the previous exercises did you find EASIEST? Why?

_____
_____
_____
_____
_____
_____
_____
_____
_____
_____
_____
_____
_____

Which of the previous exercises did you find MOST CHALLENGING? Why?

_____
_____
_____
_____
_____
_____
_____
_____
_____
_____
_____
_____
_____

Continued...

What did you discover about yourself as it relates to your writing? Focus on the positive, as well as the challenges.

_____

_____

_____

_____

_____

_____

_____

_____

_____

_____

_____

_____

_____

_____

Which, if any, of this first group of writing assignments could be expanded upon for inclusion in a book or blog? Why do you think these have value for you or your audience? (If there weren't any good candidates, that's okay, too! Just archive your work. You never know... maybe they'll be useful someday.)

_____

_____

_____

_____

_____

_____

_____

_____

_____

_____

_____

_____

Continued...

Do you plan to make any changes to how you approach the next assignments? If so, what are those changes?

_____

_____

_____

_____

_____

_____

_____

_____

_____

_____

_____

_____

_____

How are you feeling about your writing skills and progress after this batch of writing exercises?

_____

_____

_____

_____

_____

_____

_____

_____

_____

_____

_____

_____

_____

END OF WRITING PROGRESS UPDATE #1

11. What major holiday would best celebrate what your business does? Why?

12. What types of clients or customers are most difficult for you? What tips would you suggest to a colleague facing a similar scenario?

13. Imagine your business is a superhero (with or without cape and tights). How does your business save the world?

_____

_____

_____

_____

_____

_____

_____

_____

_____

_____

_____

_____

_____

_____

_____

_____

_____

_____

_____

_____

_____

_____

_____

_____

_____

_____

_____

_____

_____

_____

_____

_____

_____

14. If you could go back in time and restart your business or career, what would you do differently? How would that change have affected you?

_____

_____

_____

_____

_____

_____

_____

_____

_____

_____

_____

_____

_____

_____

_____

_____

_____

_____

_____

_____

_____

_____

_____

_____

_____

_____

_____

_____

_____

15. What are some of the stupidest things people in your business and industry do? Why are these things considered stupid?

16. Do you believe that luck played a part in making your business what it is today? Why and how did it make your business what it is?

17. What is the worst business advice you've ever received? How did following it affect your business? Why did you think it was a good idea at the time? How could you avoid making that mistake again?

18. What frustrates your clients most about buying your service or product? What have you done (or what could you do) to lessen that frustration? This is not to be a sales pitch! This is finding new ways to assist customers and clients in understanding your business' offerings.

19. What has been the highlight(s) of being in business for you? Why?

20. What future technology (whether it currently exists in theory or not) could eliminate or enhance your business? How would you best prepare for that scenario?

21. Do you believe that messiness is a sign of genius or insanity? Why? What do your customers or colleagues believe about this? Is there a disconnect between your perception and that of others? How could any disconnect be affecting your relationships with others?

22. Describe your most embarrassing business moment and how that shaped you or your business into what it is today.

23. What one word best describes you or your business? Why? Would your customers or colleagues agree? Why or why not?

24. Does your business sell a product or service with a technical component (equipment, software, Internet service, etc.)? Does this present challenges to buying? How would you address those challenges?

25. Do you believe that business is (or should be) fun? How does that affect the way you run your business?

WRITING PROGRESS UPDATE #2

Can you believe you're already a quarter of the way through the program? Go You! Take a few moments to assess how you're feeling about your progress at this point.

Which of the exercises since the last update did you find EASIEST? Why?

_____
_____
_____
_____
_____
_____
_____
_____
_____
_____
_____
_____

Which exercises since the last update did you find MOST CHALLENGING? Why?

_____
_____
_____
_____
_____
_____
_____
_____
_____
_____
_____
_____
_____
_____
_____

Continued...

What did you discover about yourself as it relates to your writing in these exercises since the last update? Focus on the positive, as well as the challenges.

_____
_____
_____
_____
_____
_____
_____
_____
_____
_____
_____
_____
_____
_____

Which, if any, of the writing assignments since the last update could be expanded upon for inclusion in a book or blog? Why do you think these have value for you or your audience? (If there weren't any, just archive your work for future reference.)

_____
_____
_____
_____
_____
_____
_____
_____
_____
_____
_____
_____
_____

Continued...

Do you plan to make any changes to how you approach the next group of assignments? If so, what are those changes?

_____

_____

_____

_____

_____

_____

_____

_____

_____

_____

_____

_____

_____

_____

How are you feeling about your writing skills and progress after this batch of writing exercises since the last update?

_____

_____

_____

_____

_____

_____

_____

_____

_____

END OF WRITING PROGRESS UPDATE #2

26. Did your college education relate to what you do today? If yes, how has it helped you (or not)? If it doesn't relate, what made you decide on a different path and how did you gain the additional knowledge you needed?

27. What is your biggest time waster at work? Does it relate to your work or not? What would prompt you to eliminate it from your day?

28. Do you have a lot of competitors that are like you? Or does competition for your business come from unlikely sources? List competitive forces you face in your business and how you handle them.

29. What causes people to drop out of your industry or career? Why have you stuck with it? And what would you say to encourage or discourage a colleague about leaving it?

30.   What does your daily schedule say about who you are and what you value?

31. What former technology or business practice have you been sorry to see go the way of the dinosaur? Why? And how could you recapture the essence of it in a new way?

_____

_____

_____

_____

_____

_____

_____

_____

_____

_____

_____

_____

_____

_____

_____

_____

_____

_____

_____

_____

_____

_____

_____

_____

_____

_____

_____

_____

_____

_____

_____

32. It's been said that people often don't implement what they learn from going to seminars or workshops. Why do you think that happens? What advice would you give for getting more value from these events?

33. Do you believe successful people in your industry are born or made? State your position and explain why you believe this way.

34. Are you a role model for your colleagues or customers? Why or why not? How does this affect your business?

35. Finish the following sentence: I cannot live without _____ in my business. Why is this so important to you? What would you do if it, whatever it is, is suddenly gone or becomes irrelevant?

36. Describe a completely unrelated event that could have a profound effect on your business or industry. How would it affect your business or industry?

_____

_____

_____

_____

_____

_____

_____

_____

_____

_____

_____

_____

_____

_____

_____

_____

_____

_____

_____

_____

_____

_____

_____

_____

_____

_____

_____

_____

_____

_____

_____

_____

37. Which mealtime is best for networking with a client or colleague? Breakfast, coffee, lunch or dinner? Why?

38. Do you think business is a game, sport or battlefield? How does this affect how you run your business?

39. Have you ever had an "aha" or "eureka" moment? What did you discover? And how did it change you or your business?

_____

_____

_____

_____

_____

_____

_____

_____

_____

_____

_____

_____

_____

_____

_____

_____

_____

_____

_____

_____

_____

_____

_____

_____

_____

_____

_____

_____

_____

_____

_____

_____

40. When a customer doesn't pay money owed you, how does that make you feel? How do you deal with those feelings?

_____
_____
_____
_____
_____
_____
_____
_____
_____
_____
_____
_____
_____
_____
_____
_____
_____
_____
_____
_____
_____
_____
_____
_____
_____
_____
_____
_____
_____
_____
_____
_____
_____
_____

41. What is the strangest thing you've done to improve your career or business? What impact did it have? And would you do it again? Why or why not?

42. What fairy tale or nursery rhyme best describes your business or career? In what ways does it relate?

43. Business clichés are everywhere, for example, "think outside the box." Which ones annoy you the most and why?

44. Businesses are often approached by charities for donations of time, talent and treasure. What prompts you to donate... or not?

45. Do you believe inbound or outbound marketing works best? How would you defend your choice?

46. What's the best day of the week for you or your business? What makes it that way? How could you make your worst day of the week better?

47. You've just time traveled to an ancient civilization (Egyptian, Roman, Greek, Norse, Incan... pick your favorite!). What would your business or career be in that culture and time? Which of your modern day skills would be used in that scenario? How?

48. Leadership is one of the most used, and often misused, terms in business. What does leadership mean for you and your business?

49. Do you give your personal mobile phone number to anyone who asks for it? Why do you or don't you?

50. The Internet has created a demand for 24/7/365 availability. Should a business be always available? Or should business hours be established? Defend your position.

WRITING PROGRESS UPDATE #3

WOOHOO! Whether you've adopted a daily or weekly writing regimen, you've made it through half of the program. Kudos on what you've accomplished so far!

Which of the exercises since the last update did you find EASIEST? Why?

_____
_____
_____
_____
_____
_____
_____
_____
_____
_____
_____
_____

Which exercises since the last update did you find MOST CHALLENGING? Why?

_____
_____
_____
_____
_____
_____
_____
_____
_____
_____
_____
_____
_____
_____
_____

Continued...

What did you discover about yourself as it relates to your writing since the last update? Focus on the positive, as well as the challenges.

_____

_____

_____

_____

_____

_____

_____

_____

_____

_____

_____

_____

_____

Which, if any, of this group of writing assignments could be expanded upon for inclusion in a book or blog? Why do you think these have value for you or your audience? (If there weren't any, simply archive for future reference.)

_____

_____

_____

_____

_____

_____

_____

_____

_____

_____

_____

_____

Continued...

Do you plan to make any changes to how you approach the next assignments? If so, what are those changes?

_____

_____

_____

_____

_____

_____

_____

_____

_____

_____

_____

How are you feeling about your writing skills and progress after this batch of writing exercises since the last update?

_____

_____

_____

_____

_____

_____

_____

_____

_____

_____

END OF PROGRESS UPDATE #3

51. What does being a team player mean for you in business? Answer even if you work for yourself.

_____

_____

_____

_____

_____

_____

_____

_____

_____

_____

_____

_____

_____

_____

_____

_____

_____

_____

_____

_____

_____

_____

_____

_____

_____

_____

_____

_____

_____

_____

_____

_____

_____

52. Do you believe that there are secrets to success? Would you be willing to share your success secrets (not proprietary or confidential information of course!) with the world? Why or why not?

53. How has the Internet and ecommerce impacted your business?

54. If you could create the perfect mastermind group, who would be in it? Anyone—
including fictional or famous—is eligible to be in your group. Why do you want
these characters in your group?

55.   Is your business "green" or environmentally friendly? How? And why?

56. Describe how social media impacts your business. If it doesn't, why doesn't it?

57. At what age do you plan to retire? Or do you plan to work until you die? Why have you made this choice?

58. Is your mobile phone a necessity or a nuisance? Why?

59. Have you ever "gone with your gut" in business? How did that turn out if you did? Would you rely on it again? Why or why not?

60. How do you feel about advertising? Helpful or hurtful? Defend your position with examples.

_____

_____

_____

_____

_____

_____

_____

_____

_____

_____

_____

_____

_____

_____

_____

_____

_____

_____

_____

_____

_____

_____

_____

_____

_____

_____

_____

_____

_____

_____

61. What would you describe as a "business meeting from hell?" Why is that scenario problematic for you?

62. Describe both the best and worst use of PowerPoint presentations and explain why you feel that way.

63. What does being creative or innovative mean for your business or industry?

64. What do you do to avoid burnout at work?

65. Does your business have a casual day? (Might be every day for those that work at home!) How does it impact your work or business if you do?

66. What would you say to encourage a high school student to pursue a career in your industry?

67. If you were stranded on an island, what essentials would you need to run your business? Why would you need these things?

68. One million dollars has just been deposited into your business bank account as a gift that you don't have to repay, except for any applicable taxes. What would you do with it?

_____
_____
_____
_____
_____
_____
_____
_____
_____
_____
_____
_____
_____
_____
_____
_____
_____
_____
_____
_____
_____
_____
_____
_____
_____
_____
_____
_____
_____
_____

69. Do you believe it's better to bootstrap or borrow to build a business? Why do you believe that?

70. What is the one thing you most want to outsource in your business? What would outsourcing that function help you accomplish?

71. How would you describe "business etiquette?" Give examples.

72. A call from an unknown caller or phone number comes in on your mobile phone. Do you answer it? Why would you or wouldn't you?

73. Should you ever turn a hobby into a business? Why or why not?

74. Were your parents, or other influential adults in your childhood, entrepreneurs, business owners or successful career professionals? Whether they were or weren't, has that affected your career? What impact did their level of success have on you?

75.   What do you do to combat work stress?

_____

_____

_____

_____

_____

_____

_____

_____

_____

_____

_____

_____

_____

_____

_____

_____

_____

_____

_____

_____

_____

_____

_____

_____

_____

_____

_____

_____

_____

_____

_____

_____

_____

WRITING PROGRESS UPDATE #4

You're three-quarters of the way through the program already! Keep going… you're heading into the home stretch!

Which of the exercises since the last update did you find EASIEST? Why?

_____
_____
_____
_____
_____
_____
_____
_____
_____
_____
_____
_____
_____
_____

Which exercises since the last update did you find MOST CHALLENGING? Why?

_____
_____
_____
_____
_____
_____
_____
_____
_____
_____
_____
_____
_____
_____
_____

Continued...

What did you discover about yourself as it relates to your writing since the last update? Focus on the positive, as well as the challenges.

_____
_____
_____
_____
_____
_____
_____
_____
_____
_____
_____
_____
_____
_____

Which, if any, of this group of writing assignments could be expanded upon for inclusion in a book or blog? Why do you think these have value for you or your audience? (If there weren't any, simply archive for future reference.)

_____
_____
_____
_____
_____
_____
_____
_____
_____
_____
_____
_____
_____
_____

Continued...

Do you plan to make any changes to how you approach the next assignments? If so, what are those changes?

_____

_____

_____

_____

_____

_____

_____

_____

_____

_____

_____

_____

_____

How are you feeling about your writing skills and progress after this batch of writing exercises since the last update?

_____

_____

_____

_____

_____

_____

_____

_____

_____

_____

_____

_____

_____

END OF WRITING PROGRESS UPDATE #4

76. Do you think work/life balance can ever be achieved? What does "balance" mean for you?

77. What is your most productive time of day: morning, afternoon or evening? How do you use or ignore that natural rhythm in your business life?

78. What does "climbing the corporate ladder" mean in today's business environment?

79. How do you deal with distractions during your workday? How's that strategy working for you... or not?

80. A client prospect wants to work with you, but you don't have the ability, resources or desire to work with them. How do you handle that scenario?

81. Describe what good customer service means for your business or industry. How is your business living up to that standard?

82. How do you believe a salesperson's personal image and demeanor affects the sale? Why should—or shouldn't—it be a factor in sales success?

83. When you were in grade school, what did you want to be when you grew up? Are you that today? What elements of that childhood dream exist in your career today, if any?

_____

_____

_____

_____

_____

_____

_____

_____

_____

_____

_____

_____

_____

_____

_____

_____

_____

_____

_____

_____

_____

_____

_____

_____

_____

_____

_____

_____

_____

_____

_____

_____

84. What does "good communication skills" mean to you?

85. Is your personality or personal style typical or atypical for your business or industry? Does that help or hinder your success?

86. How would you define "personal brand?" What is your personal brand?

87. Without naming names, describe an uncomfortable sales experience (buying or selling) you've ever had and what made it that way. Did you have anything to do with how that played out? (Be honest!)

88. Complete the following overused joke prompt: How many (job title of people in your industry or job function) does it take to change a light bulb? And why is that so?

_____

_____

_____

_____

_____

_____

_____

_____

_____

_____

_____

_____

_____

_____

_____

_____

_____

_____

_____

_____

_____

_____

_____

_____

_____

_____

_____

_____

_____

_____

_____

89. Is your business more art or science? Provide examples to illustrate.

90. Will your industry or profession be around in 50 years? What are you doing now to future-proof your business?

91. How does public speaking make you feel? Why do you think that is?

92. What trends (society, pop culture, political, tech, etc.) do you watch for your business? Why do you feel these are relevant?

93. How do you deal with the unexpected in your business?

94. How have you used networking for sales and marketing? Discuss its effectiveness and impact on your business.

95. Which do you find more effective for networking: Online or in person events? Why do you feel that way?

96. How is your business dealing with generation gaps (i.e., Millennials versus Baby Boomers)? How does that coping strategy impact your sales and/or human resource functions?

97. Freelancing is becoming a widely accepted career path for many. How has this impacted your career or business? How could you capitalize on the trend or minimize any of its negative effects?

98. Would you hire someone, as an employee or independent contractor, that was exactly like you... or different? Why?

99. If there was a natural disaster or other crisis in your area, would that represent an opportunity or a threat for your business? What would you do to adjust to your new business reality?

100. Where is your industry, business, product or service in the product life cycle (birth, growth, decline, dying)? How does that impact your profitability and plans for the future?

_____

_____

_____

_____

_____

_____

_____

_____

_____

_____

_____

_____

_____

_____

_____

_____

_____

_____

_____

_____

_____

_____

_____

_____

_____

_____

_____

_____

_____

_____

_____

101. By writing and self publishing, you have announced to the world that you want to be known as a thought leader. How does that make you feel? How do you think your influence will impact the world?

_____

_____

_____

_____

_____

_____

_____

_____

_____

_____

_____

_____

_____

_____

_____

_____

_____

_____

_____

_____

_____

_____

_____

_____

_____

_____

_____

_____

_____

_____

_____

_____

_____

_____

WRITING PROGRESS UPDATE #5

YOU MADE IT! Congratulations for sticking with it and reaching this milestone on your path to writing blogs and books for business. Time to celebrate and reflect on what you've accomplished and what you want to do next. After completing this update, move on to the next section of the book to discover how to continue your writing journey.

Which of the exercises since the last update did you find EASIEST? Why?

_____
_____
_____
_____
_____
_____
_____
_____
_____
_____
_____
_____

Which exercises since the last update did you find MOST CHALLENGING? Why?

_____
_____
_____
_____
_____
_____
_____
_____
_____
_____
_____

Continued...

What did you discover about yourself as it relates to your writing since the last update? Focus on the positive, as well as the challenges.

_____

_____

_____

_____

_____

_____

_____

_____

_____

_____

_____

_____

_____

_____

Which, if any, of this last group of writing assignments could be expanded upon for inclusion in a book or blog? Why do you think these have value for you or your audience? (If there weren't any, simply archive for future reference.)

_____

_____

_____

_____

_____

_____

_____

_____

_____

_____

_____

_____

_____

Continued...

Now that you've come to the end of these exercises, how do you plan to maintain your writing skills?

_____

_____

_____

_____

_____

_____

_____

_____

_____

_____

How are you feeling about your writing skills and progress now that the program is over?

_____

_____

_____

_____

_____

_____

_____

_____

_____

BEST WISHES FOR WHAT'S NEXT
ON YOUR WRITING JOURNEY!

ABOUT HEIDI THORNE

Dr. Heidi Thorne, MBA/DBA, is the author of several books and audiobooks on business and self publishing available on Amazon and Audible. She also has been an active blogger since 2010, and is the host of *The Heidi Thorne Show* podcast.

Heidi is a seasoned marketing professional with over 25 years of combined experience in sales and advertising, and was a trade newspaper editor for over 15 years. In addition to two advanced business degrees, Heidi also has five years of experience teaching at the college level.

To learn more about Heidi, visit **HeidiThorne.com**.

www.ingramcontent.com/pod-product-compliance
Lightning Source LLC
Chambersburg PA
CBHW081113180526

45170CB00008B/2827